Royalty

Teresa Hutton

authorHOUSE®

AuthorHouse™
1663 Liberty Drive
Bloomington, IN 47403
www.authorhouse.com
Phone: 1 (800) 839-8640

Published by AuthorHouse   05/24/2016

ISBN: 978-1-5246-1092-0 (sc)

Print information available on the last page.

Mirror mirror on the wall

When I'm happy you are discouraged

When I'm discouraged you are embraced with happiness!

When I'm looking my worst you are laughing at me.

When I'm looking my best you are still laughing at me.

Now I could be you, I could get pleasure out of
peoples uncomfortable circumstances

That of what you have said has held me back

On part it is my own fault that voice inside of my head has possessed me.

I am Free!

The words that you use against me won't faze me because I'm indestructible now!

He called on me and I fought back

Although I lost plenty of battles I won the war!

You tell me that you love me

You are a con, shallow, selfish demon.

I will speak the truth, the truth that you don't want others to hear

I'm not the one being fake the fake one is you.

I will seek for the truth and the truth is I am that demon

For, I am my worst Critic.

What is acting black?

What is acting black?

Saying ain't, Yo, Nigga, what up dog, pippin with an
accent to go along with our ignorance

What is acting black?

The mentality of a child mixed with no sense of stability,
lacking compassion and intelligence.

What is acting black?

My sistas fake weave and nails, her flamboyant personality.

What is acting black?

My brotha's baggy jeans and with a swagga to match.

What is acting black?

Well I'm black and I am smart,

I will dance to the beat of all kinds of music

I love my food of all kinds

Most of all I carry myself with an inspirational class.

So what now? Do you degrade me? Belittle me? Do
you think like the rest of the world?

I stand here to say I'm black and proud!

Heaven vs. Hell

The shadows are near, my head is spinning.

Darkness is quiet, I feel at peace.

Yet, ashamed that I am excited.

Death creeps inside me.

What do I do?

I can't see! I can't speak!

My mind is dizzy.

My soul cries.

I'm cold, Help me! He's coming.

I'm back! I see my mother for her smile is the light!

I see my father for his wisdom and love is my ears eyes, and mind.

I see my lord and savior who are my Spirit and Soul.

He called on me and I fought back.

Satan tried to take me and the lord said "No Satan you can't have my child".

The lord then carried me back to the kingdom which is heaven.

The truth is what I tell

So trapped in our own ignorance that we cannot see when we are being ignorant.

The truth what I tell

Babies dying of hunger

Fathers leaving women and children to fend for themselves.

The truth is what I tell.

Women giving themselves to men, then feeling
disrespected when they are treated like dirt

The truth is what I tell.

Children having children

The truth is what I tell.

What I thought was the truth was not

Sometimes what is wrong may be right

Sometimes what is right may be wrong.

These are all the truths of your world, my world

Maybe one day we can overcome these issues until that time comes

The truth is what I tell.

Divided nation

Divided by hatred

Divided by arrogance

Divided by Self-pity

Divided by stupidity

Yet, we stand here and say united we stand.

What is up with this infatuation of shallowness?

To be so distasteful and wasteful.

My world I see cannot cope with what is the truth

We stand here and say united we stand
Can we overcome this selfishness?

Can we remain true to ourselves?

Can we appreciate others from other ethnic backgrounds?

Can we stand strong and tall?

Can be have compassion for others?

Saying united we stand starts with oneself and ends with a nation.

Love

Love

Happiness, Pain

Fights, adventures, parties

Children, families, reunion

Love is complicated

Heart

Inspiration of a mother

I'm fifteen and argue with my mom

She says I'm a pain, but she's a bigger one

Maybe because I'm fifteen that has a lot to do with it

Through her sassiness, through her get me this, get me that

She has a smile of inspiration!

I dare not tell all for I'm supposed to be a pain!

So keep smiling mom with a smile of inspiration.

Daddy's Girl

He says I mean

I say he's a complainer

He says I'm beautiful

I say he's lying

He lectures me day and night

I listen with a sigh

If he left this world I would be lost without a sight

Daddy, Daddy, Daddy, Daddy

Please give me four kisses goodnight

Free Verse

Dancing with the wind

I want to laugh like the thunder

I want to have happiness in my life

Going to college I'm really scared of

I want to sing on stage like Mariah

When I turn around and look back at my life I want to say I

Danced with the wind.

The Dove

The dove was not ordinary

He always went as he came

He would come in the night

The dove saw me that very night

I was scared instantly of his sight

It came over fast and steady

To give a smile that was not scary

Everlasting

An everlasting is green

On the outside it is plain

It does not grow for perfection, only from the inspiration of other plants

No matter what kind of weather it comes across its growth is strong

Are you an everlasting?

No matter what life throws at me, I always rise above my own expectations

I will succeed, I will accomplish, I will Live, Laugh, Love

Color

Purple- The color for peace and serenity

Blue- The color that is very common

Yellow- The color that stands and walks with pride

Orange- The misfit that doesn't blend in

Red- The color of sweet apples, with delicious desires

Brown- The very inspiration of my skin

When you combine all these colors you get a clouded rainbow

A rainbow that makes the best color of all

Who I am

I cannot change my style

I cannot change who I like

I cannot comprehend every detail of life

I will seek to comprehend what I don't understand

My destiny is fulfilled at times

Sometimes it is wise and strong!

Other times irritating

I cannot or wouldn't dream of changing my heritage

I would rather be thick than skinny

I would rather have short hair than no hair

I would rather have wide hips than no hips

Trust that I am level headed

I am proud to be a virgin

It is not what you do, but how you do it

I am sassy, wise, short, thick, kind, mean, beautiful, and intelligent

This is me! Take me as I am!

Blossom

The girl that receives all the oohs and aahs

Is never truly seen for her flaws

She has a high IQ in education

Yet, her IQ in life is not an infatuation

The boys go wild when they see her

She secretly envies this girl named blossom

Blossom never receives the oohs and aahs

She is always seen for her flaws

Blossom doesn't realize she is the other girl's envies for her "flaws".

The boys would never admit she is hot on their list

Blossom hangs her head in shame, for she thinks her face is lame

Why am I'm not pretty she ask? How come I'm disliked?

You are not putting out her father says, trust you are beautiful.

Blossom you are intelligent, beautiful, kind, humble, funny, goofy, and groovy!

Girls all over the world you are truly blossoms! Love yourself and believe.

Pearls within a Diamond

If I had a diamond, if you had a pearl

If we went to the mountain to together

Would you stay loyal to me?

If I was four feet tall, if you was 6ft "3"

Would you carry me on your shoulders?

If you knew I was the one, would you listen to your heart
or would you shun me till the end of time

What if I was to die tomorrow, would you hold me?

Would you cry? Would you say I love? Would you believe in my faith?

I would love you till the end of the time.

The lord walks for me, never allowing me to falter

My strength is in him not you

I praise him until the end of time

This love I would sacrifice for him

If I had a diamond, if you had a pearl

Would we go to the all the way to the top together

Would you still be loyal to the end?

Thank you lord (Goodbye past)

In the night when I'm feeling tired

I listen to the sound of the steps

Reminiscing about my sins

Then I hear the lord's voice

He speaks to me with love in his heart

I am his child. He loves me no matter what!

I rejoice because I want to go with Jesus when he comes

When the tears begin to fall I feel something lightening up my heart my spirit.

I want to be saved and my heart cries out for repentance

He loves my soul

I so in love with him

I will follow you and no other

Thanks for your love always

You are my salvation!

Empress Geisha

By the tone of her voice

By the switch of her hips

The high pitch of her laugh

It is the mixture of the clouds

Geisha is her name, the artist in sight

She dances with grace

Her posture is strong

Brown eyes made of cinnamon

Tall as the sky

She is geisha to her house, but empress of a nation

She sings with the wind and dances with the wolves

Plays the instruments for the heavens and earth

Raindrops fall from the sky for mourning of her love

Geisha is her name, the artist in sight

The tenderness of silk

The strength of an army

Mother Nature to our wilderness

Queen to our seas

First Love

First loves are the memories of your heart

The build of your character

Your adolescent rebellion

They are your weaknesses and strengths

The tone of your mood

The laughs of your heart

The headaches in your mind

The food in your stomach

Your kindness for blindness

First loves give you tunnel vision

Everything is black and white

Then the time comes when you bury your first love

They go bye bye

Then another love develops

You go on round two, but through it all

You remember those playful nights

Those long phone calls

Your first "I love you"

Your first breakup

Your first makeup

The first time

Then the final break up

In time you will heal

Sometimes still reminiscing over what could have been

Then you laugh and say "Why was I crying over that person"!

You will have come a long way and will not want to turn back

You will never forget your first love

Break Free

What do I want?

I want to live to love

Spend my life with someone that wants to love me back

Be held at night with sincerness in his heart

Caressed with tenderness

Is it you? Is it me?

I want to break free from you

Haven't gotten past the curiosity

More fantasy than reality

I want to break free

Hush now Hush now Hush now

You knew this day was coming

Did you believe that I was going to live in LaLa Land?

To believe in your existence

Not anymore, I believe in my existence

We will ride together

We will die together

Spend our live together

I break free

Eagle Flying

What's this smile you have?!

What's this new attitude that has formed?!

When did you start going to church?!

Tell us Eagle, Tell us

I surrendered my life to God!

When I hear the name Jesus! I have to shout!

He puts pep in my step, I moving forward not backwards.

I am so in love with him I stand in a wide long gaze.

I don't want to be left behind when Jesus comes.

He has a plan for you as well!

This is not going to last long!

You're a party girl! You like to club!

To drink some Bacardi, Hennessey, and Old E!

You'll be back on our side in no time.

No I won't chickens; I'm going with Jesus when he comes!

Royalty (who I was, Is Not who I am)

In the darkest hours of the night I sit with tears in my eyes

Afraid to voice out loud my deepest desires, fears, and confusions

I battle myself with unforgettable thoughts of who I was

Who I was is not who I am

The girl that would speak her mind no matter what the cost

Is now the woman that considers all aspects before
she voices words that cannot be erased

The girl that did not care if you loved or disliked her

Is the woman that more cautiously chooses her friends wisely

The girl that was a tom boy

Is now the woman who dresses for Success

The girl that would cuss and fight when constantly pushed

Has learned to humble herself and to let things roll off her back

Who I was is not who I am

The woman that I am now is full of excitement in her heart

Who I am is the woman that holds her head up high

Who I am is human

I make mistakes, I get frustrated at times, I get attitudes,

Who I am is funny, smart, sensitive and beautiful

The girl and woman are both of great value

Who I was is not who I am

Always In Reach

As I sit and listen to the birds chirping

The steadiness in the day, the soulful laughs in the neighborhood

I see myself amongst them all, wondering all in my thoughts

The radio starts to play Faith Hill's "There You'll be"
and I start singing to the top of my lungs

This song brings acknowledgement to my heart

I remember when I when I was upset you brought a smile to my face

When I slid off track, you willed me back in

You loved me when my hair was all over my head, clothes
were not presentable, and my status wasn't Ms. "IT"

You claimed acceptance of me when others urged you to walk away

You told me I was beautiful when my mind told me I was shameful to look at

You held my hand and patted my back when everyone was around

You ALWAYS say "I love you" truthful to the bone

You have treated me better than I have treated myself

You are always encouraging in everything I do

You showed up to all my events and loudly cheered me on

You'll always be there to show me unconditional love

No matter happens I know you are just a call away

A Woman She is, A Phenomenal Woman

When she walks into the scene her look is impressionable

From the way her lips curve into a sweet smile that draws you near

The way her eyes challenge the look of the unknown

A look of ambition, excitement and future goals

The woman is the solid factor to the undeniable

But the misconception is the newest of the fools

Undeniable woman she is with her posture strong

Untamable Spirit for her heart lingers on

Daring to the one who challenges her soul

Faithful to the Love that is inside of her heart

But the Girl inside her screams to be louder Louder LOUDER LOUDER

Until the girl is gone and the woman is whole

Foolish girl she was lingering on hopeless desires

Untamable spirit she had when she believed a deceiver's tales

The girl cried to get out of the body

She jumped out ready to step into all the future holds

Now the woman that stands in the light entering the room

Is not questionable about who she is

Accepting everything with Grace and humbleness

Going beyond measure to touch and believe the unknown

Slaying her own expectations one by one

Phenomenal woman that is clothed right

Vivacious woman she is, that marches to her own drums

Intelligent woman she is, that speaks with elegance

Spiritual woman she is that keeps GOD NUMBER ONE

Humble woman she is that has such a genuine virtue

Fire Cracker woman that will roar when her loves are in danger

Loving woman that will soften the most roaring mean lion

Stylish woman that is not afraid to embrace her empowerment

Glory of a woman that impacts all that she comes across

She is whole, she lives life, she is strong that builds in Love

Phenomenal woman she is, one of the best in sight!

Enraged

When I look back and see what I saw, I seen that
my eyes were shaded, sealed not to fall

When I think about all the time that was given for me to
move around and not keep my head in the clouds

The manipulation of Words that came from the mouth
are the words that haunted my heart

Looking back putting the pieces together, realizing
there was never anything to put together

Only for me to take the blinders off, to face what I never wanted to face

Cause my heart was so pure towards the heart of the other that
I put my guard down and since wanted to shudder!

And I can't take it back ...trust that I gave without hesitation

And I can't take it...the love that was unconditional

And I can't take it back...the conversations where I told my soul

And I can't take it back...the feeling's I held

And I can't take it back...The Friendship that was one sided

Enraged with you I thought you did me harm

Blindsided from truth that set me free

And I cried cried cried day and night for long periods of time

Cause the person I knew never existed

Never captured my heart of hearts

Cause the true person I've been enraged with is myself

That I played myself with bad characteristics that were shown from the beginning

And I won't take it back... because trust is for the future

I won't take it back...because love goes to the end

I won't take it back.... Friendship is real

When I thought about the humiliation of my tunnel vision I failed

I grew from the experience; though I was enraged I looked in the mirror

And the mirror pointed back at me ....

Enraged clouded my judgment to be real with myself...

Enraged no longer, but stronger from the acts ...Enraged a delusion of us.

Dream

Time Racing, Drums beating, Sound Loud, and deep obsession

Nothing is postponed for the time has come

To devour that fear and take what is yours

The wind is strong as it hears the boldest chant

Dream Day and Night

For Dreams have no time limit

Dream all the time cause dreams bring a vision

Take a Stand and step out from the dream that hides behind the cloud

Sound the Drums louder for the time is NOW

The moment is NOW

The Dream is loud waiting to COME OUT!!!!!!!

But it is not going to become a reality until you get up and DO

Dream big, Dream loud, Dream strong cause there is no harm

Follow your dreams and Sound the alarm!

Friendship

Meeting you I was so non chalant with no expectancy
that we would endure a journey

Who would've thought that we would become inseparable

Crying together

Laughing Together

Fighting together

Achieving Success together

The bond has become so strong that I dare not stumble to a huge fall

Because I know that in that fall you would hurt for me all the way to the end

I know that you would rise up and with your sword
protecting my heart that would fall

When people said I was nothing you spoke to the pureness of who I am

When they counted me out you tripled your numbers on me

When those that professed to have loved me turned their
backs on me, you held out your hand to catch me

There were times I did fall and hard I fell with a shame
that was replaced with nonjudgmental eyes

Do you not know the importance you carry, if you left my side

They say Never say Never

Never will I be the same

Never will I will have a friend as great as you

A love that touches my soul

That whisper's to me in the middle of the night

That touches my dreams so sweet and pure

And I won't let you down, because you carried me so high

Always a phone call away, when you begin to lose sight

Friend always Day and Night

Summer and spring

Fall and winter

Through tears of Joy

Through Tears of Sorrow

No other like you comes to mind

Friendship that is Everlasting

The Truest in Sight!

Roar of a Lion

I smile

I walk

I glide

I strut

With a quietness that is unknown

Looking from side to side scoping out those that
think I'm unaware of the unknown

The smile tells a tale that flaws truly know

But the eyes smile with love and when needed ready to war

I Smile because I know what it is not to

I walk with Grace because past years of shame

I glide because I used to glide like a fool

I strut because I know one of the best is entering

Oh but don't let the assumption of this smile let you be blinded

That I won't roar when you step in my zone

Don't let that walk, have you thinking foolish thoughts

That glide gets you to jumping

Don't let that strut have you laughing in arrogance

The strength that rises is nothing less than you think

The smile is peace that is always lighting the atmosphere

But when needed be the lion comes out to roar

It stands firm, loud, strong and focused

When the roar is lost in the sounds of quietness

That smile comes again because I know where I've been!

But now, I yawn because I know they don't know

The Roar of a Lion

Party Anthem (Celebration)

Ready Ready Ready Ready Shout

Stepping out tonight

Ready to hit the door

Got my smile and dancing moves

Cause when they see me coming

They already know!

When it's time to dance (DANCE)!

When it's time to Laugh (LAUGH)!

Let them know whose boss (BOSS)!

Cause when I step in my zone, I'm shining!

Shining Bright and right

Music is loud and vibing

The beat matches the vibration of my hips

Dip low, slip and slide, front to back

When it's time to dance (DANCE)!

When it's time to laugh (LAUGH)!

Let them know whose boss (BOSS)!

I came to have fun (FUN)!

Good vibes all the way around

Living life to the fullest

Celebrating all night long!

Go getter (Coming for what is mine)

I woke up feeling like, it's time to get on down

To own what is mine

Predestined for success

Celebrating all the Boss's

That does their thing and owns it

Realizing myself too, it's time to make those moves

To rise on up

Show on up

Giving my all

To the dream inside

Will walk like it's mine (cause it is)

Will speak it into existence (because it's time)

To rise on up

Shown on up

To the purpose of my life

Boss's never quit, even when they stumble

Boss's always make a way

They always press on

Always winning

So I'm coming to rise on up

To show on up

To the dream that is mine

Because the time has come

To grab what is mine!

I can feel it

I can feel it

When it's not right

I can feel it

When I need to press harder

I can feel it when it's not just a moment

I can feel it

Because my body trembles

Shakes me to the soul

I can feel it

When I need to go far

I can feel it

When I need playtime

I can feel it

When it's me

I can feel it

Knowing I haven't go past the curiosity

I can feel it

I can feel it

I can see it

I can show it

I can watch it

I can hear it

I can feel to the bottom up

Fast lane

We Rhode fast and high

Not thinking about what tomorrow would bring

The money, cars, and power we had!

We did it big, with the looks from all over the world

It was good

It was exciting

Cause sin was fun

And fun we did have

With no limits cared for

cause it was what it was

anyone that stepped in our presence may have
not liked us but always respected us

Any sucka that tried to front on us was three rights out of their lane

We thought we had more years to be about this life

Until the feds came crashing down with every snitch that envied us

And the fast lane we left

Calling every friend in sight

Oh sin was fun until we got caught

But now we doing big time

Who wants to come start a fight

In the Fast lane we were and all was good

Until the feds came crashing down

They knew we were up to no good!

A Mother's Wish

It was like heaven when mama held me

When she wiped away my tears

Saying baby don't cry, mama still here

And I held her tight

Not to lose her again

When she picked me up and said baby girl be strong

mama won't let anyone do you harm

And years later I still hear mama loud and clear

Saying baby I love you so dear

Saying if only you knew mama would die for you

And faded you did into a memory that is not forgotten

I can't help that I still weep for you to be near

Mama taught me strength

Strength that was unknown

To soar and fly chasing after my dreams

You wished me the best

For me to live life to the fullest

And always give my best

Mama I'm grown now and still need you near

But always know baby girl was listening

You are always there with me to break the chain

To take the challenge and press on

You taught me to be a boss and move on

Not letting any male define who I am

You encouraged me to love God and say my prayers

Mama you are always near and in my heart

I will fulfill a mother's wish

Always There

Everytime I came around it was something always there

Something I could never shake off

Intuition told me something wasn't right

That I needed to boss out

Say bye bye

And I fought to say intuition was a lie

But that thought was always there

When you said your cared (was it the truth or a lie)

When you smiled at me (was it the truth or a lie)

But I see very clear now

Intuition was always there

Liar liar pants on fire

Intuition told me the truth

But I lied to myself

So I'm the liar because I didn't listen to my intuition

It was always there!

Oh she seemed so flyyyy!

When she said your name you just lit up

When she agreed with what you liked, you had to hit her up

She switched, agreed, laugh and used her loving to trance

And a fool you became

Not ever remaining the same!

In a trance you were for you were locked on her

Cause she spelled you up with sex being her love

In love you were as a fool sexed will be

But it all came crashing cause sex will not keepth thee!

Oh she seemed so fly when she smiled at thee

Oh she seemed so fly when you told her everything

Oh she seemed so fly when you trusted thee

But now you looking like a fool cause love wasn't in thee!

So when you look for the next know that trance

When you reject the best remember you would have never been kept

When she talked the talked and didn't walk the walk

Remember seemed so fly

Cause you let true love pass you by!

Printed in the United States
By Bookmasters